NIGHT GAUNTS

AN ENTERTAINMENT BASED ON THE LIFE AND WRITINGS OF
H. P. LOVECRAFT

by
BRETT RUTHERFORD
*with additional
Poetica Lovecraftiana*

GRIM REAPER BOOKS
Providence, Rhode Island

Copyright © 1993, 2005 by Brett Rutherford
All Rights Reserved

Excerpts from Sonia Greene Lovecraft's Memoirs
adapted with permission of Necronomicon Press
Frontispiece photo of Carl Johnson as H.P. Lovecraft, by Keith
Johnson.

Second edition, revised, 2005
Second printing, 2008
ISBN 0-922558-16-7

GRIM REAPER BOOKS
are published by
THE POET'S PRESS
279-1/2 Thayer Street
Providence, RI 02906
www.poetspress.org

This book is also available on CD-ROM
in Adobe Acrobat format.

ABOUT THIS BOOK

THE FIRST DRAFT of this play was written as a special commemoration for the 50th anniversary of Lovecraft's death. It was written after I attended a ceremony organized by Carl Johnson, a Rhode Island-born actor and Lovecraft fan. A few days later, still delighted with having met some of the eminent Lovecraft fans face-to-face for the first time, I wrote the poem, "At Lovecraft's Grave," and conceived the idea of publishing the poem as a chapbook.

As I had recently done with a book of poems by Edgar Allan Poe and Sarah Helen Whitman, I also envisioned a publishing party in which actors would bring Lovecraft back to life. This, of course, required a script, which turned out to be a more substantial undertaking than the poetry chapbook.

The Providence Athenaeum was enthusiastic about hosting the event, an ideal setting since Lovecraft lived across the street just before his death in 1937. A one-hour first draft of *Night Gaunts* was created, and a cast of professional actors and actresses and readers assembled. We chose the March 15th weekend of 1988 for the premiere — a time chosen to coincide with the next annual visit of Lovecraftians to Providence.

Carl Johnson, who had personally undertaken the local memorial program for Lovecraft, turned out to be an actor well suited to play the role of the Old Gent. His make-up and demeanor startled and delighted all of us. Two fine actresses brought to life Lovecraft's mother and wife: Rose-Anna Semich was Susan Phillips Lovecraft and Susan Bowen was Sonia Greene. The disembodied voices in the script were performed by Stuart Blazer, Pieter Vanderbeck, and Brett Rutherford.

The staged reading, on Sunday March 13, 1988, was sold out, and the work was well-received, as was the chapbook published that day, *At Lovecraft's Grave.* That limited edition is now unavailable. Ironically (or characteristically), the New York HPL fans, for whose pleasure the work

5

was specially crafted, did not attend. They were off on a side trip in rural Rhode Island, perhaps in search of the Dark Swamp.

The 90-minute, two-act version of *Night Gaunts* was written for the Lovecraft Centennial year in 1990. It was performed in a staged reading at The Providence Athenaeum on Tuesday, September 30, of that year. Carl Johnson recreated his role as Lovecraft and Susan Bowen returned for a much more extensive portrayal of Sonia. The role of Lovecraft's mother was so admirably acted by Kristen Marie Hardy that I wrote an extra "mad scene" for her as the Act One curtain. The voices were played by Robert North, Pieter Vanderbeck and Brett Rutherford. In both productions, the recorded voice of Lovecraft's mother was performed by Eileen McNamara, and the voice of the child Lovecraft by Charles Denby.

The longer version of the play was well-received by a sold-out house.

At the time of this new printing (2002), Lovecraft's fiction is now being printed in several rival editions, one stemming from the original Derleth Arkham House version and the other from S.T. Joshi's "definitive text," also first published by Arkham House. An "Estate of H.P. Lovecraft" is also cited on some copyright pages, but it seems almost a certainty now that Lovecraft's fiction has all entered the public domain. The full text of all of Lovecraft's fiction and poetry is now widely distributed on the Internet. Nonetheless, to avoid any possible conflict with anyone claiming to own dramatic rights to any Lovecraft story, the playwright limited his use of Lovecraft's fiction to excerpted passages, not acted as a story line but presented to demonstrate and illustrate Lovecraft's literary style. In other words, no stories by Lovecraft are dramatized here.

Lovecraft's dialogues and monologues in this play are based partially on his letters, the rest on an imaginative reconstruction of his conversation based on his known mannerisms and habits. The text contains scores of Lovecraft "sound bites," mostly from the Arkham House selected letters volumes edited by August Derleth and Donald Wandrei. These are woven together with material of my own devising to create the impression of an evening spent in the company of this wonderfully eccentric man. If I have succeeded, the boundary between Lovecraft's letters and my conjectural speeches should be seamless.

The dialogue of Sonia is based, with permission, upon her actual memoirs, as published by Necronomicon Press.

I will confess, too, that I made a character study of Frank Belknap Long and his Russian Jewish wife, Lyda, during my close acquaintance with them during Frank's declining years. He was so like Lovecraft in temperament, and so influenced by HPL as a young man, that it was not hard to see an element of hero worship and imitation in his personality, including his choice of a dominating and polar opposite mate. I always felt, in visiting with Frank and Lyda, that I was seeing what Lovecraft and Sonia might have become as a couple in old age — not a pretty picture.

After this play's first limited edition publication, several reviewers misunderstood my purpose in breaking up some sections of dialogue into lines that resemble poetry. This was not an attempt to rewrite Lovecraft as poetry (and in fact the passages used verbatim are scarcely altered). This instead is an attempt to give the actor a *phrased* text, which will make for easier sight-reading and quicker memorization. No other purpose was intended in this way of presenting the actors' lines. The actors in both staged readings found this very helpful.

The script of this play can also be performed as a radio play with little or no adaptation.

The poem, *At Lovecraft's Grave*, and several other Lovecraft-related pieces, are included at the end of this book. I have been gratified and honored to see that readings of these poems, and re-enactments of tidbits from this play, have become regular occurrences at Lovecraft's grave side in Swan Point. I include these poems in this book since some of them have become ceremonial or even theatrical in their own right, and I encourage others to use them.

BRETT RUTHERFORD
Providence, January 2005

DRAMATIS PERSONAE

HOWARD PHILLIPS LOVECRAFT

MALE VOICE #1
Narration of fiction and poetry
Male gossip #1; Doctor

MALE VOICE #2
Narration of fiction and poetry
Male gossip #2; Priest

MALE VOICE #3
Narration of fiction and poetry
Madman's monologue from "The Rats in the Walls"
Banker

SUSAN PHILLIPS LOVECRAFT,
Mother of H.P. Lovecraft
MAY ALSO DOUBLE
FEMALE VOICE #1
Narration of fiction and poetry
Female gossip #1
Nurse
Screaming woman (Nahum's wife)

SONIA GREENE LOVECRAFT,
Wife of H.P. Lovecraft
MAY ALSO DOUBLE
FEMALE VOICE #2
Narration of fiction and poetry
Female gossip #2
Nurse

CHILD'S VOICE
(heard on tape recording only)

ACT ONE

MUSICAL PRELUDE as house lights dim and dim stage light reveals:

SETTING: Sitting room of the home of Howard Phillips Lovecraft. The winter of 1936-37. Lovecraft is seated in a winged chair, next to him a small antique table of Georgian design with an unlit lamp, a stack of writing paper and pen and ink. There is a simple wooden chair or stool behind the desk. Various papers litter the floor where they have been carelessly dropped. A porcelain tea service sits neglected on a silver tray on the floor next to the table. Draped over another chair is a long, English-style overcoat. Books are everywhere, on shelves and in stacks on the floor.

The back of the stage contains one door. One window with interior shutters at stage right.

Lovecraft, seated in the upholstered chair, is writing a letter, squinting in the dimness of dusk light. He does not turn on the lamp. He pauses, puts down the pen, and leans back in the chair. His hand moves into his threadbare jacket to clutch his stomach and he grimaces in pain. He leans back in the chair and closes his eyes; his other hand drops toward the floor.

(The stage darkens during the following.)
(SOUND EFFECTS: Wind — flapping wings — bird calls. A child screams, waking from a nightmare.)

SUSAN LOVECRAFT
(Opening door and running into child's room.) Howard! Child, what is it?

CHILD'S VOICE
It was them again, Mother — the Night Gaunts. They carried me away.

11

SUSAN LOVECRAFT

Have you been into those gothic novels of your grandfather's again? Haven't I told you to mind your lessons instead? See what those awful books do to you!

CHILD'S VOICE

No, Mother, it wasn't the books. Or even a dream. They were real. There were dozens of them, black and rubbery. They had wings, and talons. They carried me through the air, tossed me like a toy from one to the other. They were taking me to their nest in the mountains.

SUSAN LOVECRAFT

You silly boy. It's midnight. You can see the windows are locked, the curtains are drawn. Not even a ladybug could get in here. You're just thinking of those crows you saw last summer — and that dead thing they were picking away at. It upset you so.

CHILD'S VOICE

These were not crows, Mother. They were *Night Gaunts.* I know that's what they're called. They have bat wings, and long tails.

SUSAN LOVECRAFT

(Insistent) It's just your imagination … *(Soothing)* My poor, precious Howard … just those filthy crows.

CHILD'S VOICE

(Agitated) No, they aren't like birds at all. They don't have beaks. They don't even have feathers. I saw them as clear as day. In fact —

SUSAN LOVECRAFT

(Irritated) That's enough, Howard. You'll ruin your health with these incessant nightmares.

CHILD'S VOICE

(Doggedly) In fact, Mother, they were so close, I could see the reptilian scales on their heads. And they had no faces ... NO FACES AT ALL!

SUSAN LOVECRAFT

(Alarmed) Howard! .... *(A pause, as Mother turns aside and moves away from Howard's bedside. She is speaking to someone in the doorway.)* What can we do for this boy, Annie? I have to look after him every moment. He's so sensitive. And such a homely child — every time I look at him I see his father. Whatever will become of him? *(A pause.)*

CHILD'S VOICE

(Quietly) Mother?

SUSAN LOVECRAFT

(Returning to the bedside.) No more, Howard, please.

CHILD'S VOICE

Mother, will it happen to me, too? Is that why I see the Night Gaunts? Is it happening already?

SUSAN LOVECRAFT

Is what happening?

CHILD'S VOICE

Will I go insane like Father? Will they take me away to Butler Hospital, too?

SUSAN LOVECRAFT

(Distinctly, aloof.) We will not ... speak of that. What happened to your father will not happen to you. Or to me. Now go to sleep.

CHILD'S VOICE

But the Night Gaunts —

SUSAN LOVECRAFT

There are no Night Gaunts. No monsters, Howard. We don't have to have monsters. Men and women are quite bad enough already. The way they gossip and cheat and lie. In two years it will be 1900 and men are still no better than savages. Now, no more about your Night Gaunts...they are *not real.*

(Mother closes the door. A pause... The boy shifts in his blankets and sheets...wind and wing beats...Lights up. Lovecraft turns on the lamp and reads from the letter he was writing:)

LOVECRAFT

I have not seen the Night Gaunts since those nightmares thirty-four years ago. What a journey! They carried me through infinite leagues of black air, over the towers of dead and horrible cities. Up we would go, into a gray void, so high that mountains miles below would be pinnacles like needles. Sometimes, when we arrived there, they would toss me back and forth.

I wondered who built the cities, and from whence came the strange, piping flutes and drumbeats. That was years before I dreamt of the Elder Gods and their cities. It's as if the Night Gaunts already were leading me there, showing me the territory.

(Sighs, picks up pen.) But when I was eight I grew interested in science and cast off my last shred of religion and other superstitious belief. Oh, I was well prepared for it — I knew my letters at two and was reading at four. By my venerable eighth year I had been through hundreds of tomes from Grandfather's library. The classics paganized me — the Age of Reason civilized me.

(Puts down pen, folds and seals letter in envelope. He picks up a stack of sealed envelopes on the table and counts them.)

That's ten letters today. A poor showing ... at least five more epistles need answering. How many have I written — eighty thousand, maybe a hundred thousand? What a hecatomb of papyrus! I've frittered away my time on correspondence, a dreadful vice, although not nearly as painful as my verse.

(Quotes, with his hand raised and in a formal tone.) "Mature as moonshine Booze, and free from Bunk as the frank Perfume of the candid Skunk." Still, I have had my moments...

MALE VOICE #1

Out of what crypt they crawl, I cannot tell,
But every night I see the rubbery things,
Black, horned and slender,
    with membranous wings,
And tails that bear the bifid barb of hell.
They come in legions on the north wind's swell
With obscene clutch that titillates and stings,
Snatching me off on monstrous voyagings
To grey worlds hidden deep
    in nightmare's well.

MALE VOICE #2

Over the jagged peaks of Thok they sweep,
Heedless of all the cries I try to make,
And down the nether pits to that foul lake
Where the puffed shoggoths
    splash in doubtful sleep.
But oh! If only they would make some sound,
Or wear a face where faces should be found!

LOVECRAFT

Ultimately, science is more important than poetry. The poet is not a prophet. He is in truth more often wrong than right, since he is always led by unreliable sympathies and caprices. Who could effect a more perfect formula for human misery than the poet who asserted that "Beauty is Truth, and Truth, Beauty"?

The steel-cold man of intelligence — not the glowing bard — is the one who gets the closest to the truth — the question of what *is* and what *isn't*. Poetry and art are for beauty — science and philosophy are for truth.

I should know about the folly of poetry. In my teens and twenties I did little else. My nights were divided between amateur astronomy and the writing of Georgian verse. My days were spent in sleep, or in skull-wracking seizures of migraine. The headaches came often — three times a week. For days I lay like Roderick Usher, unable to bear light, crouched beneath pillows to avoid the slightest noise.

My nocturnal world kept me away from the tawdry commercial life of the city — the begetting of money and the rattling nuisance of delivery trucks and repairmen. These seemed to exist only as a footnote — as the least important, autonomous events underpinning a gentlemanly life.

My childhood seemed to have been designed to make me an outsider. My mother was talented — more spirited by far than my more conventional aunts — but she would not hear of me associating with the common lot of children. *(Closes his eyes)*

MALE VOICE #1

There's that boy in the garden across the street. The one who never plays.

FEMALE VOICE #2

You say he hides when the other boys come along?

MALE VOICE #1

Yes, that's what he does. And he always has a book.

FEMALE VOICE #2

Do the other boys torment him? He looks so delicate!

MALE VOICE #1

They never bother him. They hardly see him. He hides behind those shrubs.

FEMALE VOICE #2

This summer he had a tent there. I went over and talked with him. He said he had become an Arab and was learning sorcery.

MALE VOICE #1

Ah, *The Arabian Nights!* Harmless enough. We all read them as boys.

FEMALE VOICE #2

He is so clever. He even made up an Arabic name for himself — Abdul Alhazred. And he was writing in a most beautiful hand — the old fashioned kind of writing we learned in school.

MALE VOICE #1

Ah, there's his mother come to fetch him. She's so pale.

FEMALE VOICE #2

That's the arsenic.

MALE VOICE #1

Arsenic?

FEMALE VOICE #2

(Quieter) She eats arsenic to keep her complexion pale. She could easily marry again. Her father has a considerable fortune. It was tragic what happened to that family.

MALE VOICE #1

Winfield Scott Lovecraft. A traveling man. Dissolute. Health ruined, family ruined.

SUSAN LOVECRAFT

Where is that boy? *(Calling)* Howard! Howard! *(Pauses)* There you are. I told you not to go outside the garden. You know the other children can't bear to look at your face. And put that book back in your grandfather's library. The bright sun isn't good for the leather bindings. Then go up to your room and your Aunt Annie will bring you some milk. And take that towel off your head.

LOVECRAFT

When I was a boy I sometimes overheard things I was not meant to know about. I thought the answers were in books, but there were subjects so taboo that generations had devoted themselves to clever circumlocutions. It's hard to image that the simple plumbing of human reproduction can still only be described in Latin. I did not always understand, but through my voracious reading I soon gained an adult's comprehension of the things that men and women do. Standing behind a door I heard my mother and the family doctor...

MALE VOICE #1 (DOCTOR)

(Steps forward from chorus and addresses Mother.) Mrs. Lovecraft, I have troubling news for you.

SUSAN LOVECRAFT

Tell me, doctor. Spare me nothing. Will Winfield recover?

MALE VOICE #1 (DOCTOR)

He will live. He has not had any hallucinations since we brought him back from Chicago. He could live for some years yet, but he will not recover.

SUSAN LOVECRAFT

Whatever do you mean? Will he be an invalid? Is he mad?

MALE VOICE #1 (DOCTOR)

We must watch him closely. The disease has overtaken his system. I fear the paresis is rather advanced.

SUSAN LOVECRAFT

(Pauses, hesitating.) You said, the disease. What do you mean, precisely?

MALE VOICE #1 (DOCTOR)

(Clearing his throat) There are certain classes of diseases, madame, which we are very reluctant to speak of. I am very embarrassed to name them before a lady in her own home.

SUSAN LOVECRAFT

And Winfield has contracted this ... this ... condition.

MALE VOICE #1 (DOCTOR)

I'm sorry. There can be no doubt. Winfield Scott has had it for some time.

SUSAN LOVECRAFT

For how long?

MALE VOICE #1 (DOCTOR)

A year, two years perhaps. I hate to be indelicate, but it will be necessary to examine you and the child. The germ you see, is spread — it is passed ...

SUSAN LOVECRAFT

(Rearing up) I know perfectly well how these things are spread, Doctor. Every educated woman knows. I assure you no examination will be necessary. He did pass this thing from me, nor did he pass it to the child.

MALE VOICE #1 (DOCTOR)

Still, it would be prudent.

SUSAN LOVECRAFT

(Shrilly). No. (A pause) Doctor, he has not touched me — not since Howard was born. I could not bear it. *(Turning away)* These are things no one should speak of, but there, I have said it.

MALE VOICE #1 (DOCTOR)
If you are absolutely certain, I will not insist.

SUSAN LOVECRAFT
I had letters telling me of Winfield's ... adventures. Right here in Providence, and in Boston. After a while he made no secret that there had been many. He was unrepentant. From the moment I knew —

MALE VOICE #1 (DOCTOR)
I ascertain your meaning, Mrs. Lovecraft. You protected yourself. I cannot tell you in how many houses — on this very street, even — the doors are closed at night between husband and wife.

SUSAN LOVECRAFT
And there is no cure?

MALE VOICE #1 (DOCTOR)
Sometimes we can effect a treatment with metallic salts if the disease is caught early. But once the brain and nerves are affected ... paresis... blindness ... madness ... death. *(Shakes his head.)*

SUSAN LOVECRAFT
You will take him to the hospital, then?

MALE VOICE #1 (DOCTOR)
To Butler, Mrs. Lovecraft. It will be a permanent commitment.

SUSAN LOVECRAFT
My father will provide for it, then.

MALE VOICE #1 (DOCTOR)
Although, we could arrange for him to be cared for at home....

SUSAN LOVECRAFT

No! *(Looks back and forth nervously as though being watched by all the neighbors at once).* No, it would be better for everyone concerned. No one must see him this way. The selfish, wretched man … he has ruined us all. *(Mother and the Doctor fade back into the Chorus.)*

LOVECRAFT

So Father vanished onto the grounds of Butler Hospital. We visited — at first, often — then, as his condition worsened, my mother would not take me. Then he was dead. I did not see the body — just the box being lowered into the earth at Swan Point.

During the months after his burial, I bicycled out to Swan Point frequently, always ending up at the Phillips plot. The bicycle would take me right to it like a dowsing rod. I suppose I shall wind up there myself one day.

There is a fine spreading beech tree there. I would climb it, studying the grave site from the overhanging branches. I was reading Poe, then, and I imagined that I heard the muffled screams as Father revived in his coffin. But he never did.

Although the Phillips house was wonderful, the idyll did not last. My grandfather's fortune declined. (His dam in Idaho collapsed — he built another — and then *it* collapsed.) Servants and luxuries were cut back.

Gramp's sudden death meant the closure and sale of the palatial manse. We moved a few blocks away to Number 598 Angell. A modest apartment, rented, sans servants and brow to brow with pestiferous neighbors.

I watched Mother and Aunt Annie go through the library, boxing books for the auction. It gave me a shiver on Gramp's behalf. He once told me, "If there's anything worse than dying, it's having your library sold off!" All those eighteenth century treasures — gone forever!

FEMALE VOICE #1

There he is again! See him over there sitting on the steps of the Phillips house? Doesn't he know they don't live there any more? Doesn't he know it was sold when Whipple Phillips died?

FEMALE VOICE #2

He goes there every day after school. Refuses to go to his own house. He just sits on the porch steps, as if he expected someone to come and hand him the keys—give him the house back.

LOVECRAFT

We had a small settlement. The proceeds from my father's estate, from Gramp, and from the sale of the house were prudently invested. But somehow my mother became obsessed with the fear that we would one day be indigent.

Had these calamities not pressed in on us, I might have made that natural progression to become a man of letters. While my schooling was irregular — Mother and the family doctor kept me out for several years — I still might have gone on to Brown and from thence to some scholarly nook.

God knows I would have been at home among those wheezing ancients who teach Greek and Latin — those unreconstructed classicists — although I would have been shunned by my fellow students with their penchant for booze and bad Socialism.

You smile at my scorn for the radicals? My friends think me an *ordinary* conservative. I am no such thing. Most people are conservative because they have a morbid terror of doing their own thinking. I am a conservative because I am a cynic and a pagan. Christianity as the mob practices it is pretty repellent stuff—just a Jewish cult that indulges in symbolic cannibalism.

I once thought of a life devoted to astronomy. Astronomy is a pure and clean and rational thing. I was spared the drudgery and mathematics and saw only the sheer adventure of it. I bicycled up to Ladd Observatory where I was permitted to observe the movements of the moon, the planets, the stars. Although I was still a mere child, several newspapers carried my astronomy columns, penned and by-lined by H.P. Lovecraft. I especially enjoyed debunking that appalling and frivolous pseudo-science called astrology.

MUSIC CUE #2 (A portion of the Overture is replayed on a celeste while the Voices intone the following names resonantly:)

MALE VOICE #1

Aldebaran!

MALE VOICE #2

Rigel!

FEMALE VOICE #1

Betelgeuse!

MALE VOICE #1

Antares in the Scorpion!

MALE VOICE #2

The shimmering Pleiades mourning their vanished sister!

FEMALE VOICE #1

Cold Arcturus who shattered the sleep of Mrs. Whitman!

MALE VOICE #1

Implacable Orion, reeling above Poe as he lifted the bottle of laudanum...

FEMALE VOICE #2

Sadly this star I mistrust! *(Music ends).*

LOVECRAFT

Poe and his Helen were obsessed with certain stars, too. I wrote a little verse called "Astrophobos" about how the neutral and eternal stars can become an object of horror.

FEMALE VOICE #2

Crimson burned the star of madness
As behind the beams I peered,
All was woe that seemed but gladness
Ere my gaze with Truth was seared.

Cacodaemons, mired with madness
Through the fevered flickering leered.

MALE VOICE #2
Now I know the fiendish fable
That the golden glitter bore;
Now I shun the spangled sable
That I watched and loved before;
But the horror, set and stable,
Haunts my soul forevermore!

LOVECRAFT
A man of science should blush to hear such lines quoted back to him. And yet it was in the realm of the fantastic — the eldritch and terrible — that I was to gain what pitiful renown I have enjoyed. I peopled the earth with Cthulhu and the Elder Gods — unspeakable obscenities banished here by the Great Old Ones. Another monster — He Who Is Not to Be Named — dwells in the Hyades. A race of great telepathic beings live on Yuggoth, the black trans-Neptunian planet that astronomers had yet to discover.

Six years ago a young fellow from Kansas discovered the ninth planet. His name was Clyde Tombaugh and they called the planet Pluto. I think Yuggoth is still more suggestive of ice and distance and cold, don't you? *(Pause.)* At least they didn't name it Clyde.

Still, the stars were clean and uncomplicated. Next to them what I love best is Providence itself. *(Opens window for a moment and gazes out, then closes the shutter.)* Not the *people,* mind you — I have little contact with *persons* — but the city as it exists from the hours of twilight until sunrise. This is the pure Providence — history as architecture — which I can explore as a traveler might turn over the stones of a necropolis...not what man *is* — a teeming, nasty, hive-like creature — but what he builds and leaves behind.

I wrote a letter which *The Providence Journal* published a while back, protesting the idea of demolishing the brick row of warehouses along the river downtown. Someday people will come to understand that architectural coherence is the soul of a city.

FEMALE VOICE #1

Howard was a rationalist, a keen eighteenth century mind. And yet when he picked up his pen he could make a post office — a laundry — the waiting room of a doctor's office—any mundane human dwelling — sound like the vestibule of hell.

MALE VOICE #2

I've had a letter from Howard today. Just listen to this:

MALE VOICE #1

Providence is in truth a more extensive,
varied and colorful city than I had ever suspected,
and I mean to see more of its curious wonders.
There is much of the ancient waterfront
     to explore —
the east front
where all the houses and warehouses are Colonial,
and the west front
where Colonial vestiges
lurk furtively amidst the factories,
   coal-pockets and gas-works.
We walked to the southerly section
west of the Great Bridge,
    around Richmond and Chestnut Streets,
now sunk to slums...
Here indeed I found a world of wonder!
Not a stone's throw
from the traveled business section,
tucked quietly in behind
Broad and Weybosset Streets,
lurk the beginnings of a squalid Colonial labyrinth
in which I moved as an utter stranger,
each moment wondering
whether I was in my native town,
or in some leprous, distorted
witch-Salem of fever or nightmare.

This ancient and pestilential reticulation
of crumbling cottages and decaying doorways
was like nothing I had ever beheld
save in dream—
it was the 18th century of Goya....
I wandered up hills
where rotting Doric columns
rested on worn stone steps.
Rusted footscrapers rose like malignant fungi.
Dirty, small-paned windows
leered malevolently,
and sometimes glasslessly,
from gouged sockets.
There was a fog,
and out of it and into it again
moved dark monstrous, DISEASED shapes.
They may have been people,
or what once were,
or might have been, people....

FEMALE VOICE #2
Here's a new tale by that Lovecraft fellow ... the Providence recluse.
It's called "The Shunned House." Listen to how it begins:

FEMALE VOICE #1
Edgar Allan Poe came here
to woo the poetess,
Mrs. Sarah Helen Whitman,
in 1848 and 1849.
Poe generally stopped at the Mansion House
    on Benefit Street —
the renamed Golden Ball Inn
whose roof has sheltered
    Washington, Jefferson and Lafayette —
and his favorite walk led northward

along the same street
to Mrs. Whitman's home
and the neighborhood churchyard of St. John's,
whose hidden expanse
of eighteenth century gravestones
had for him a peculiar fascination.
In this walk, so many times repeated,
the world's greatest master
of the terrible and the bizarre
was obliged to pass a particular house
on the eastern side of the street;
a dingy, antiquated structure
perched on the abruptly rising side-hill,
with a great unkempt yard...

MALE VOICE #2

In my childhood
the shunned house was vacant,
with barren, gnarled and terrible old trees,
long, queerly pale grass,
and nightmarishly misshapen weeds
in the high terraced yard
where birds never lingered.
We boys used to overrun the place,
and I can still recall my youthful terror
not only at the morbid strangeness
of the sinister vegetation,
but at the eldritch atmosphere and odour
of the dilapidated house,
whose unlocked front door was often entered
in quest of shudders.
The small paned windows were largely broken,
and a nameless air of desolation
hung round the precarious paneling,
peeling wallpaper,

falling plaster,
rickety staircases,
and such fragments of battered furniture
as still remained.
The dust and cobwebs
added their touch of the fearful,
and brave indeed was the boy
who would voluntarily ascend
the ladder to the attic....
But it was the dank, humid cellar
which somehow exerted
the strongest repulsion on us,
even though it was wholly above ground
on the street side,
with only a thin door
and window-pierced brick wall
to separate it from the busy sidewalk....
For one thing,
the bad odor of the house was strongest there;
and for another thing
we did not like the white fungous growths
which occasionally sprang up
in rainy summer weather
from the hard earth floor.
Those fungi,
grotesquely like the vegetation
in the yard outside,
were truly horrible in their outlines;
detestable parodies
of toadstools and Indian pipes...
They rotted quickly,
and at one stage
became slightly phosphorescent;
so that nocturnal passers-by
sometimes spoke of witch-fires

glowing behind the broken panes
of the foeter-spreading windows....

    (MUSIC CUE #3. The sound of bells, playing the main theme from the Overture.)

LOVECRAFT
Mother began to decline markedly —

FEMALE GOSSIP #2
I saw Susie Phillips Lovecraft on the Butler Avenue Streetcar today. We were only three blocks from her house and she cried out —

SUSAN LOVECRAFT
(Alarmed) Where am I? What is this place? I don't know where I am!

FEMALE GOSSIP #2
It was most alarming. One poor old man looked as if he would leap off the car. Susie kept shrieking until the conductor got someone to walk her home.

MALE GOSSIP #1
She stands in the hedges by the house at dusk. She says that's when THEY come out.

LOVECRAFT
She began to fancy that creatures of a vague and indefinable nature emerged at dusk from the corners of her room. She developed a complete obsession about light and geometry. Furniture and draperies were moved, lamps thrown helter skelter, but still they intruded. Finally it became necessary to — *(Pauses, lowers his head with a pained expression)*

FEMALE GOSSIP #2

Have you heard about Susie Lovecraft? She's been committed — to Butler Hospital! Just like her husband before her! The poor family! That poor young man!

MALE GOSSIP #2

It may run in the family, you know. We should keep an eye out.

(Howard crosses to the edge of the stage. Mother leaves the chorus and they walk together, ending at the rear stage door.)

SUSAN LOVECRAFT

Howard, you don't look well. You haven't been eating properly.

LOVECRAFT

I'm fine, mother. Aunt Annie is a fine cook.

SUSAN LOVECRAFT

But I'm sure she doesn't bring you milk, the way I always do when you stay up writing all night.

LOVECRAFT

She tries to do everything exactly as you would want it, Mother. Look at the swans on the Seekonk over there.

SUSAN LOVECRAFT

It's cold here, Howard. It's getting much too late in the year to meet here on the grounds. You've never come into the building.

LOVECRAFT

(Maneuvers her toward door.) I'll walk you to the door. Later I'll send some flowers, and some of those chocolates you asked for —

SUSAN LOVECRAFT

I'd forsake all that if you would just come in. The room they have given me is most unsuitable. It gets dark much too soon in the afternoon and the lamps are inadequate. You know I must have the light to keep THEM from getting through. Oh, do come in, Howard.

LOVECRAFT

Mother, you know...I...cannot.

SUSAN LOVECRAFT

(Growing agitated.) I've been here for a year and a half. You've never come in.

LOVECRAFT

Aunt Annie comes in. I call every day. We have delightful walks here.

SUSAN LOVECRAFT

If only you could *see* them, Howard. The way they hide in the shadows, moving in and out so no one else can see them. They'll be there as clear as can be, and then when the nurse comes, they shuffle off into the shadows. They're so wily.

LOVECRAFT

I must be going now, Mother. We're almost to the door. *(They reach the door. Mother backs into the doorway, Lovecraft holds back.)*

SUSAN LOVECRAFT

(Receding into doorway, as if attendants are pulling her in.) They wait until the room is dark. When there's a moon I can barely feel them, just the ends of their fingers grazing against my cheek. On a moonless night they become solid. They hurt me, Howard — *(Lovecraft closes the door on her with an expression of anguish.)*

MUSIC CUE #4: CONFUSED BELL SOUNDS. Lovecraft crosses stage to window during the music.

LOVECRAFT

(Brokenly) She told everyone there about her son the poet. If she had only recovered from her surgery, she might have ultimately returned home. We could have looked after her.

FEMALE VOICE #2

Lovecraft has a tale in *Amazing Stories* this month. It's called "The Colour Out of Space." It's about the aftermath of the fall of a meteorite on a New England farm.

MALE VOICE #1

After the meteor fell...
the word passed from mouth to mouth—

FEMALE VOICE #2

There's poison in Nahum's ground!

MALE VOICE #2

The trees budded prematurely...
and at night they swayed ominously
in the wind.
Nahum's second son Thaddeus,
a lad of fifteen,
swore that they swayed also
when there was no wind;
but even the gossips would not credit this...

FEMALE VOICE #2

All the orchard trees blossomed forth
in strange colors,
and through the stony soil of the yard...
no sane wholesome colors were to be seen
except in the green grass and leafage...

MALE VOICE #1

The "Dutchman's breeches"
became a thing of sinister menace,
and the bloodroots grew insolent
    in their chromatic perversion...
In May the insects came,
and Nahum's place
became a nightmare of buzzing and crawling.
Most of the creatures
seemed not quite usual
in their aspects and motions,
and their nocturnal habits
contradicted all former experience.
The Gardners took to watching at night...
Thaddeus had been right about the trees...
the boughs surely moved, and there was no wind.

FEMALE VOICE #2

Toward the end of May the milk began to be bad.

MALE VOICE #2

Then Nahum had the cows driven to the uplands,
after which this trouble ceased.
No one was surprised
when the news of Mrs. Gardner's madness
stole around.
It happened in June,
about the anniversary of the meteor's fall,
and the poor woman screamed
about things in the air
which she could not describe.
In her raving
there was not a single specific noun,
but only verbs and pronouns.
Things moved and changed and fluttered,

and ears tingled to impulses
which were not wholly sounds.
Something was taken away—
she was being drained of something—
something was fastening itself on her
that ought not to be—

FEMALE VOICE #1
(SCREAMING WOMAN)

(Agitated, on the verge of hysteria) It's COLD, but it BURNS, and it sucks the life out of you...

MALE VOICE #2

Nothing was ever still in the night —
the walls and windows shifted.
Nahum did not send her to the county asylum,
but let her wander about the house
as long as she was harmless to herself and others....
But when the boys grew afraid of her...
he decided to keep her locked in the attic.
By July she had ceased to speak
and crawled on all fours,
and before that month was over
Nahum got the mad notion
that she was slightly luminous in the dark ...

SUSAN LOVECRAFT

(Stepping forward from Chorus as Lovecraft closes his eyes.) I will not consent to this surgery. I will NOT consent, doctor, unless you promise me about the lights. *(Pauses, as if carrying on a conversation.)*

Of course it's important. It's vital. I may be sleeping ... I may be unconscious ... and then anything could happen. The lights must be on at all times. At no time must those corners fall into shadow.

Something about corners? Well you wouldn't know, of course. It took me years to understand. Not just any corners, mind you. Only perfectly square corners where the walls meet the ceiling … an intersection of three planes. A mathematician could explain it …. my son Howard could explain it. Such corners are weak places, like little mouse holes. They see us through them. They watch us. If it's dark enough, they come out.

Has anyone else seen them? Howard told me he has, many times. He saw them as a child and I didn't believe him. Don't nod like that, as though you're humoring me.

Who are they? *(With growing rancor.)* They…They…THEY! Around and among us…in the dust and the dead leaves…squeezing out of corners. What do they want? Hah! What do they all want? To touch! Oh, subtle at first, like a gentle breeze. Then one day something as cold as ice tried to put its hand on me. One was in my bedclothes. Another brushed against me as I was dressing. Not shadows. Things that live IN shadows. Gaunt. Malevolent. Lustful. Filthy things, like dustrags.

(Runs her hands through her hair, leaving it in disarray.) What do they want? *(Desperately)* WHAT DO THEY WANT? *(Blackout)*

ACT TWO

(MUSIC CUE #5: Sonia's theme. Interlude.)

LOVECRAFT
(Writing a letter again) What can I say about being married — or whether one should be married? I was married for a while, as astonishing as that may seem to my friends. I can scarcely believe it myself.

Matrimony can be a very helpful and pleasing permanent arrangement when both parties share the same mental and imaginative habits. The trouble is that not even a psychiatrist could tell if two people are suitable for one another. It takes two to three years of living together to determine if you should live together. Fortunately for myself — and for Mrs. H.P. Lovecraft — divorce laws are now progressive enough to allow rational adjustments.

The Mrs. and I were very fond of one another... *(muses).*

(Lovecraft moves off the center of the stage. Sonia steps forward from the Chorus for the following section:)

LOVECRAFT
(Facing Sonia) How could any woman love a face like mine?
SONIA
(Facing Lovecraft) A mother could...and some who are not mothers would not have to try very hard.

LOVECRAFT
(Facing audience, but maintaining an awareness of her presence.) We met through the circles of amateur journalism. She was everywhere, bringing all of us scattered correspondents and writers together for tea and excursions.

SONIA

(Turning to audience, but giving Lovecraft sidelong glances at appropriate points.) I invited Lovecraft and several other writers to be my guests at my apartment in Brooklyn. It was a very daring thing in those days, and I surprised myself by inviting these men into my home. But I was determined to go ahead. *(Pauses)* Actually, I am rather inclined toward the lean, ascetic type, and I was puzzled that Howard regarded himself as such an ugly duckling. Besides, I realized his genius and felt that all he needed was encouragement and help. He could have been very successful in New York. When we were married, he looked starved.

LOVECRAFT

After a few months of domestic life I grew rather stout. Thank God I was able to lose all those pounds in a matter of weeks after returning to Rhode Island. For a while, I rather resembled an Antarctic penguin.

SONIA

Annie and Lillian were supposed to send him fifteen dollars a week — his allowance of the proceeds of the family estate. Howard and his two aunts had twenty thousand dollars, which had to last them the rest of their natural lives. They only sent him five dollars a week and in some weeks nothing at all. As I was making more than ten thousand a year as a buyer, it hardly mattered. I looked after Howard's needs and he never lacked for pocket money when our friends were in town. I even bought him new clothes —

LOVECRAFT

She even dragged me into a haberdashery and insisted on my getting a new overcoat. And then I had to have a suit, and then new trousers. My old clothes from 1918 were still quite fine.

(A momentary blackout. When the lights come on, Sonia and Lovecraft are entering through the back stage door.)

SONIA

(Rushing in.) Oh dear God, no!

LOVECRAFT

(Sleepily) What is it my dear, what's wrong? You, invoking the Deity, no less!

SONIA

Just look around you. The room's a shambles. The window is open. We've been burglarized!

LOVECRAFT

(Searching about the borders of the room.) I knew it. I knew it was bound to happen the moment you told me the landlady permitted...foreigners to board here. *(Alarmed at last.)* They've taken the radio — the radio!

SONIA

(Tearing through clothes in a closet.) Oh Howard, they've taken your suit! All your new clothes are gone!

LOVECRAFT

(Turned away from Sonia, he smiles faintly.) How very unfortunate.
(Black out. Sonia and Lovecraft return to their previous positions before the lights come up again.)

LOVECRAFT

I was actually a little relieved to lose the new apparel. Nowadays I can even wear some of my father's finely cut suits. The collars look a little strange. Obnoxious children sometimes assume I'm a gentleman of the theater and annoy me.

But I dress in keeping with the Lovecraft and Phillips honor. I'd prefer a periwig and an eighteenth century waistcoat, but that would disturb the neighbors a trifle.

Ultimately it wasn't beauty that killed the beast — it was New York itself. Trying to live there drove me close to madness. I found the daily contact with the rat-faced mongrel hordes in Manhattan abhorrent.

SONIA

I think Howard hated humanity in the abstract. When he learned that our apartment neighbor was Syrian, he recoiled like someone who had found a rattlesnake in his bathtub.

LOVECRAFT

New York is a pest hole.
Rats — millions of them —
wharf rats with tails
longer than a Chinaman's queue.
And cockroaches, my God, a living carpet of them.
But for vermin nothing can match the people:

One cannot describe the noxious miasma
of a subway car at rush hour,
or the heterogeneous horde
that shuffles through lower Manhattan
on weekends,
snuffling for bargains
among the seedy sidewalk vendors.

There are beggars so noxious and dirty
that raindrops fall sideways to avoid them.
It makes one wish that a portion of the globe
would neatly pass through a cloud of cyanogen gas.

SONIA

And yet as soon as Howard came to know someone personally, their background became irrelevant. I had to remind him that I was a Russian Jew, and he would assure me that of course I was *exceptional*. Well, I managed to show him lots of exceptions to his unthinking prejudices. I don't think there was one friend of his who wasn't a social outsider in some way. James Morton, possibly Howard's fastest friend, is a free-thinking atheist, an ardent supporter of Negro rights, who was kind enough to forgive Howard's racist mutterings. A remarkable man, and a vigorous pamphleteer. Frank Long is strangled by his mother's apron strings and doesn't know how to boil water. And Howard never seemed to figure out how close to Oscar Wilde many of his friends were, even after Samuel Loveman dragged us to a low place with Hart Crane, a bunch of drunken sailors, and some pretty seedy cross-dressers. What was actually going on just seemed to fly over Howard's head.

He was utterly unfamiliar with how other people lived. When we went to an Italian restaurant in Brooklyn, Howard admitted that he — a man in his third decade of life — had never had spaghetti with sauce and cheese. He absolutely detested seafood and connected the produce of the sea with decay and things utterly sinister.

(*Turning to Howard*) Howard, things are going to be difficult unless you receive some kind of employment. New York is a very expensive place to live.

LOVECRAFT

I know, my dear. I am working on it. While you were out today I typed ten copies of a letter soliciting employment.

SONIA

That's wonderful, Howard. And to whom will you apply?

LOVECRAFT

To the publishers, naturally. With my talents and background—

SONIA

— and your fine new suit—

LOVECRAFT

That, too. One of the companies should, as the phrase goes, snap me up.

SONIA

I'm so proud of you.

LOVECRAFT

But my dear, I should not expect to be a full-fledged editor at the start. One has to establish one's reputation for discernment, good judgment and superior taste.

SONIA

They will know all that from just looking at you.

LOVECRAFT

That is your wifely prejudice, my dear. To the rest of the city I'm a loping, long-jawed alien. Mirrors crack when I pass them.

SONIA

(Protesting) Howard, really!

LOVECRAFT

Babies cry out in terror. Dogs bristle with suspicion.

SONIA

Don't go on that way.

LOVECRAFT

I see them closing the shutters of the upper windows when I first turn the corner. I hear the mothers calling their children in.

(Suddenly, seized by inspiration, Lovecraft leaps to center stage and recites the last paragraph of "The Outsider" in the most exaggerated, Barrymore-esque manner:)

For although nepenthe has calmed me,

I know now that I am an outsider,

a stranger in this century

and among those who are still men.

This I have known

ever since I stretched out my fingers

to the ABOMINATION

within the great gilded frame;

STRETCHED OUT MY FINGERS
AND TOUCHED
A COLD, UNYIELDING SURFACE
OF POLISHED GLASS.

SONIA

Howard, stop that! You know I detest that story! *(Trying to get him off the track.)* Read me your letter, Howard.

LOVECRAFT

(Fumbles for one of the copies on the desk.) Here it is. *(Reads)* If an unprovoked application for employment seems somewhat unusual in these days of system, agencies and advertising, I trust the circumstances surrounding this one may help to mitigate what would otherwise be obtrusive forwardness. *(Takes a breath.)*

SONIA

That's very stuffy.

LOVECRAFT

One has to establish a tone of politeness. And such an opener demonstrates the complexity of my thought processes. I am not going to say — as those brutes over in Red Hook might — "Ay-yoo! Gimme a job, huh?"

SONIA

I wasn't suggesting that. But it's too indirect.

LOVECRAFT

But I get to the point. *(Reads again)* Certain definitely marketable aptitudes must be put forward in an unconventional manner if they are to override the current fetish which demands prior commercial experience.... Since commencing two months ago, a quest for work for which I am naturally and scholastically well fitted, I have answered nearly a hundred advertisements without gaining so much as one chance for satisfactory hearing —

SONIA

That will never do. You're telling the reader that a hundred others have rejected you.

LOVECRAFT

A hundred fools, O Matron of My Hearth. I am flattering my reader that he is the exceptional one. It's a matter of rhetoric.

SONIA

Do you tell them what kind of position you want?

LOVECRAFT

Naturally, it's here on page two. *(Turning the letter over and running his hand down the page, then reads)* ...author, reviser, re-writer, critic, reviewer, correspondent, proofreader, typist or anything else even remotely of the sort.

SONIA

(Looking over Howard's shoulder). And what are all those other paragraphs?

LOVECRAFT

Just elaboration.

SONIA

(Impatiently.) Let me see. *(Takes letter and speed reads, frowning. Then she reads aloud.)* "My education, while not including the university or a professional translator's knowledge of modern language, is that of a gentleman...." Oh, Howard, this just won't do.

LOVECRAFT

It will have to "do." It is my best. I cannot lie about myself.

SONIA

So embellish a little.

LOVECRAFT

I am a gentleman. I do not have a commercial nature. It is not in my ancestry.

SONIA

Your grandfather was a *businessman*. He had interests all over the country.

LOVECRAFT

He invested. He did not go on the subway to an office. He worked in his library, or he traveled to the Northwest where his dams were being constructed. The bankers called on him. The neighbors hardly knew he was in business.

SONIA

(To clinch the argument) Your father worked. He was a silver salesman. A salesman, no better than those street peddlers you so despise.

LOVECRAFT

(Becoming haughty.) He conducted his business in distant cities. No one in Providence was aware of it. He had the air of a gentleman.

SONIA

It was very damaging for you to be brought up with these expectations … living with aunts who hadn't the faintest idea how the world makes its living. They encouraged these 18th Century notions.

LOVECRAFT

Don't criticize the aunties. They admire you.

SONIA

Because I took them to lunch. And because I sent them hats.

LOVECRAFT

That's unkind.

SONIA

Annie stayed here for weeks at my apartment. We took her out every night. I never even received a thank you note. And I know they are keeping some of your share of your little income. They admire me because they think you've snagged a rich woman — and a foolish one.

LOVECRAFT

How could you suggest such a thing?

SONIA

(Going on, ignoring Howard's rage.) Well I am not a fool and I am NOT rich. I work for every penny. Everyone works today, Howard. Absolutely everyone.

LOVECRAFT

(With an air of finality, but sullenly.) A gentleman need not. An artist … ought not.

SONIA

(To herself) And a husband?

The stage is bathed in complete darkness. Howard and Sonia's voices are heard close to one another.

SONIA

It's three o'clock, Howard. I thought you'd never come to bed.

LOVECRAFT

I was revising a story. I — I thought you'd be asleep by now.

SONIA

I'm wide awake. Don't you know what tonight is?

LOVECRAFT

Tonight? I'm not sure. Wednesday —

SONIA

It's our anniversary. A year since our wedding night.

LOVECRAFT

Don't. That tickles.

SONIA

It didn't tickle then. You liked it.

LOVECRAFT

It was novel then. I was not accustomed to being touched. It is not always desirable.

SONIA

Aren't you too warm in those pajamas. Let me —

LOVECRAFT

It's a cool night. Please stop that.

SONIA

You are my husband. *(Then, obviously snuggling up to him, in Russian)* Moi moozh, moi moozh. Ya vass abazhayoo. *(A beat of silence)* Well, Howard?

LOVECRAFT

Hmm?

SONIA

Aren't you going to...do something?

LOVECRAFT

Do something?

SONIA

The way we did then.

LOVECRAFT

I think it would be better not to. I — I think I have a migraine coming.

(For a beat of silence we hear Sonia move across the room. A door opens and closes, and, from the other side of the door, Sonia's voice, sobbing.)

LOVECRAFT

At the end we could live neither there nor here. Trying to think of living in Rhode Island drove the late missus equally close to despair. She proposed to come up and open a millinery shop here, but my aunts determined—

SONIA

— determined that neither they nor Howard could afford to have a wife in Providence who *worked*.

LOVECRAFT

Sonia accepted a position with a company in the mid-West. Although I protested that we could remain married and meet now and then, she insisted on a divorce, which I was finally persuaded to consent to.

(Sonia returns to the Chorus and Lovecraft goes back to writing his letter)

I think the chances for a successful marriage for a strongly individu- ated, opinionated and imaginative person are damn slender. It's wiser to lay off after venture Number One. I remain a proud, lone entity face to face with the cosmos. A haughty celibacy is not a terrible price to pay for cerebral integrity.

(Pauses, turns to a copy of WEIRD TALES.)

Farnsworth Wright has bought a few of my stories for *Weird Tales*, and *Amazing Stories* has taken some of the others. Sometimes it seems scarcely worth the trouble of typing — I hate typing. At a half a cent a word, you learn to live on canned beans and saltines. As it is, I manage to eat on a bud- get of two dollars and ten cents a week: doughnuts, coffee with four lumps of $C_{12}H_{22}O_{11}$, a slice of cheese, two slices of Bond Bread, a can of chili or vegetable soup or corned beef hash, and a quadrant of pie.

(Puts down pen. Pauses. Picks up pen again to add:) Lately, though, I've been obliged to make that an octant of pie.

The other problem with being published in the pulps is that before you even get your copy the pages have started to turn yellow. As for a book — I've had a small book, riddled with errors, titled "The Shadow Over Innsmouth." A slovenly job. Who knows if I will ever be treated to a more elegant tombstone? Ultimately I think that only books count. If the pulp magazines pull writers down in one way, the slick magazines do so too. No one who has gone that route ever comes back to his true genius.

A fellow once offered to do "The Shunned House" as a little book. It got as far as the printing press, but never to the bindery. The unbound sheets have been drifting from pillar to post since 1928!

(Lovecraft winces in pain and goes to the chair, where he nearly collapses.)

It's nothing...really nothing. Perhaps a relapse of the digestive ills that plagued my youth...or some kind of grippe coming on. I really must get back to my stories. Suggestion is the highest form of horror presentation. The basis of all true cosmic horror is violation of the order of nature. The mob will never realize this — they want Grand Guignol and horror shows.

I have dabbled in both, of course. I wrote a pot-boiler of the most obvious sort for a little magazine called Home Brew. It was "Herbert West — Reanimator." In just a few pages it had grave robbing —

MALE VOICE #1
We followed the local death notices like ghouls....

MALE VOICE #3
Accident victims were our best hope.

FEMALE VOICE #1
The process of unearthing was slow and sordid.
FEMALE VOICE #2
The affair made us rather nervous...

MALE VOICE #3
...especially the stiff form and vacant face of our first trophy...

LOVECRAFT
...revival of the dead with West's reanimating fluid...

FEMALE VOICE #1
The awful event was very sudden...

MALE VOICE #1
...the most appalling and demonaic succession of cries...

FEMALE VOICE #2
Human it could not have been.

MALE VOICE #2
It is not in man to make such sounds.

MALE VOICE #3

We leaped to the nearest windows —

FEMALE VOICE #1

— vaulting madly into the starred abyss of the rural night.

LOVECRAFT

The home with the reanimated corpse luckily burned to the ground. West and his friend continued their work on smaller subjects —

MALE VOICE #1

The scientific slaughter of uncounted small animals...

LOVECRAFT

Then tried the fluid on a fresher corpse —

MALE VOICE #2

The thing actually opened its eyes, but only stared at the ceiling with a look of soul-petrifying horror before collapsing.

MALE VOICE #3

West said it was not fresh enough — the hot summer air does not favour corpses.

LOVECRAFT

Herbert West's nemesis was Dean Halsey of Arkham Medical School. After the good dean died, Herbert could not resist reviving the old fellow to prove to him once and for all that reanimation works...But the ungrateful dean misbehaves....

MALE VOICE #1

A terrible killing...

MALE VOICE #2
...a watchman clawed to death.

FEMALE VOICE #1
Eight houses were entered by a nameless thing which strewed red death in its wake...

MALE VOICE #3
It had not left behind quite all that it had attacked...

FEMALE VOICE #2
...for sometimes it had been hungry....

LOVECRAFT
(Smiling, but waving back the speakers) Enough! It had more carnage than King Lear. Later I learned how to be more suggestive, to create suspense and dread. Sometimes I withheld the horror until the FINAL PARAGRAPH.

MALE VOICE #1
The caller had on one of Edward's overcoats — its bottom almost touching the ground, and its sleeves rolled back yet still covering the hands. On the head was a slouch hat pulled low, while a black silk muffler concealed the face. As I stepped unsteadily forward, the figure made a semi-liquid sound...glub...glub — and thrust at me a large, closely written paper impaled on the end of a pencil.

FEMALE VOICE #1
You know how damned life-like Pickman's paintings were — how we all wondered where he got those faces. Well — that paper wasn't a photograph of just a background, after all. What it showed was simply the monstrous being he was painting on that awful canvas. By God, it was a photograph from life.

FEMALE VOICE #2

It grew fast and big for the same reason that Wilbur grew fast and big — but it beat him because it had a greater share of the outsideness in it. You needn't ask how Wilbur called it out of the air —

MALE VOICE #1

(Interrupting, with a rustic accent) Bigger'n a barn...all made o' squirmin' ropes...dozens o' legs...great bulgin' eyes all over it...ten or twenty mouths or trunks big as stovepipes, an' all a- tossin' an' openin' an' shuttin'—

FEMALE VOICE #2

He didn't call it out. It was his twin brother, but it looked more like the father than he did.

(Turns to a paper on the desk.) Ah, now here's a letter from a young fellow who's just read "The Rats in the Walls"... *(Reads quietly with a smile.)*

(MUSIC CUE #6. *Drumbeats and bass instruments play the main Overture theme.)*

MALE VOICE #3 (MADMAN)

It was a twilit grotto of enormous height,
stretching away farther than any eye could see;
a subterraneous world of limitless mystery
and horrible suggestion.
There were buildings
and other architectural remains —
in one terrified glance
I saw a weird pattern of tumuli,
a savage circle of monoliths,
a low-domed Roman ruin,
a sprawling Saxon pile,
and an early English edifice of wood —
but all these were dwarfed
by the ghoulish spectacle
presented by the general surface of the ground.

For yards about the steps
extended an insane tangle of human bones,
or bones at least as human
as those on the steps.
Like a foamy sea they stretched,
some fallen apart,
but others wholly
or partly
articulated as skeletons;
these latter invariably
in postures of demoniac frenzy,
either fighting off some menace
or clutching other forms with cannibal intent...
all the bones were gnawed, mostly by rats,
but somewhat by others
of the half-human drove.

Mixed with them
were many tiny bones of rats—
fallen members of the lethal army...
It was the antechamber of hell...
Once my foot slipped
near a horribly yawning brink,
and I had a moment of ecstatic fear.
I must have been musing a long time,
for I could not see any of the party
but the plump Captain Norrys.
Then there came a sound
from that inky, boundless, farther distance
that I thought I knew;
and I saw my old black cat
dart past me
like a winged Egyptian god,
straight into the illimitable gulf
of the unknown.

But I was not far behind,
for there was no doubt after another second.
It was the eldritch scurrying
of those fiend-born rats,
always questing for new horrors,
and determined to lead me on
even unto those grinning caverns
of earth's center
where Nyarlathotep,
the mad faceless god,
howls blindly in the darkness
to the piping
of two amorphous idiot flute-players...
Something bumped into me —
something soft and plump.
It must have been the rats;
the viscous, gelatinous,
ravenous army
that feast on the dead and the living...
They found me in the blackness
after three hours;
found me crouching in the blackness
over the plump, half-eaten body
of Captain Norrys,
with my own cat leaping and tearing at my throat...
When I speak of poor Norrys
they accuse me of a hideous thing,
but they must know that I did not do it.
They must know
it was the rats;
the slithering, scurrying rats
whose scampering will never let me sleep;
the daemon rats
that race behind the padding in this room
and beckon me down

to greater horrors
than I have ever known;
the rats they can never hear;
the rats,
THE RATS IN THE WALLS...

LOVECRAFT
(Goes to window and looks out over the Providence skyline with a pair of opera glasses.) Life in Providence is never dull. They had a riot over at Brown on Memorial Day. Poor Dean Mason had to go through the motions of expelling some of the lads for their rough-and-tumble. Bet he was damn sorry to do so — just Nordic high spirits. Here's hoping the boys do better next year.

(Raising coffee cup in a toast.) I'd love to crack skulls in the name of free individualism. They could plow up the airport, burn the Rotary club, and duck the mill owners in the most oil-polluted spot in the Providence River! *(Looks about on the desk for something to emphasize the gesture and, finally, raises a saltine cracker from the bowl on the table and cracks it defiantly in half.)*

Sing ho for simplicity, strength, lusty freedom, gentlemen's privilege, agriculture, leisure and the square-rigged India trade. Narragansett cheese and pacers, Cumberland copper, Newport spermaceti, and Cranston iron. Rum, Negroes and molasses. God save the King!

MUSIC CUE #7: *(Lovecraft stands at attention as a lugubriously slow setting of "God Save the King" plays on harpsichord. Then he pours some coffee.)*

FEMALE GOSSIP #1
Have you seen Howard Lovecraft lately — that writer who lives on College Street?

FEMALE GOSSIP #2
Why, yes, just yesterday. He looked dreadful. So pale—

FEMALE GOSSIP #1
He's always pale.

FEMALE GOSSIP #2

No, paler than before. And thin. He staggered and leaned against a telephone pole. Papers fell on the sidewalk. It took him the longest time to pick them up.

FEMALE GOSSIP #1

His aunt should get him to a doctor. Maybe we should call her.

FEMALE GOSSIP #2

I think not, dear. It's none of our concern.

MALE VOICE #3 (BANKER)

Who's that you're going on about?

FEMALE GOSSIP #1

Howard Lovecraft, dear, just a little gossip.

MALE VOICE #3 (BANKER)

Howard Lovecraft, you say? Odd, he came into the bank today. Signed off on the last note from his estate. Only five hundred dollars left to his name. You say he's ill?

FEMALE GOSSIP #2

Millie was just saying he *looks* ill.

MALE VOICE #3 (BANKER)

That's the way some of these funny old families go. Little by little they dip into their principal. Then it's gone. If they're lucky, they die.

FEMALE GOSSIP #1

Well, maybe he has something hidden away! He's a writer. He probably gets royalties...

(MUSIC CUE #8: *An eerie trio for three pan flutes plays while the stage is darkened. Lovecraft seats himself on the chair, covered with a comforter and surrounding his head with pillows.*)

LOVECRAFT

(Writing a letter) I am surely sorry to hear of your poor health, which is surely paralleled by my own. My persistent touch of grippe keeps my digestion in very bad shape, and I have no strength at all....Brief afternoon walks when it is warm enough...

Am now acutely ill with intestinal trouble following grippe...

No strength — constant pain....Bloated with gas and have to sit and sleep constantly in chair with pillows...Doctor is going to call in a stomach specialist Tuesday....

MALE VOICE #1 (DOCTOR)

(Leaving the Chorus and standing next to Lovecraft.) The time to operate would have been a year ago — a year and a half ago. I'm afraid it's hopeless. *(Shakes head and returns to Chorus.)*

LOVECRAFT

I can read and write only a few minutes at a time...taking three medicines at once.

MALE VOICE #2 (PRIEST)

(Leaves Chorus and stands next to Lovecraft.) I'm Father Delaney. The nurse told me you might like to chat.

LOVECRAFT

(Coldly) The nurse was mistaken, Father. Besides, I'm an atheist —a pagan.

MALE VOICE #2 (PRIEST)

They've told me you're gravely ill. Don't you fear for your immortal soul?

LOVECRAFT

The notion of immortality is...untenable.

MALE VOICE #2 (PRIEST)

You do not believe in a divine creation?

LOVECRAFT

(Disconnectedly) Cause and effect....a vast number of wholly unrelated causes. The universe just IS. No hocus-pocus....

MALE VOICE #2 (PRIEST)

I would like to pray for you.

LOVECRAFT

To whom? To WHAT? I am a priest, too. I MAKE GODS. Gods that would eat yours as a cat eats a mouse...Cthulhu...Yog-Sothoth....
Nyarlathotep....The Goat with a Thousand Young...*(Makes goat horns with his hands.)*

(The priest runs off in terror and returns to the Chorus.)

FEMALE VOICE #2 (NURSE)

(Leaves Chorus and stands next to Lovecraft.) Mr. Lovecraft! Look what you've done — you've driven the Father off.

LOVECRAFT

Father....Father....Yog-Sothoth! *(laughs feebly)* I suppose I'm dying. It all seems so trivial. It's not the way I imagined it. It doesn't come out of a great Eye and snatch you away. You don't get the thrill of feeling your heart pound with delectable terror. It's just pain and nurses and drugs...

FEMALE VOICE #2 (NURSE)

(Remains by Lovecraft's side and speaks to other Female Voice in Chorus) He's so brave...so stoic. He knows he's dying. He won't see the priest.

FEMALE VOICE #1

(Coming to Lovecraft's side) And he seems so grateful for everything we do for him. He's a real gentleman...the way they used to be.

LOVECRAFT

I want to dream in an atmosphere of my childhood...to sit on Prospect Terrace with an old book or a pad and pencil in my hands...

MALE VOICE #1

(Coming to Lovecraft's side.) The train sped on, and I experienced silent convulsions of joy in returning...New Haven...New London and then quaint Mystic...Then at last a still subtler magic filled the air — nobler roofs and steeples — Westerly — in His Majesty's RHODE ISLAND AND PROVIDENCE PLANTATIONS! GOD SAVE THE KING!

MALE VOICE #2

(Coming to Lovecraft's side.) I fumble with the bags and wraps in a desperate effort to appear calm — then — a delirious marble dome outside the window —

FEMALE VOICE #1

A hissing of air brakes —-

FEMALE VOICE #2

A slackening of speed —

LOVECRAFT

HOME—
UNION STATION —
PROVIDENCE!!!

There is no other place for me. My world is Providence. I *am* Providence, and Providence is *myself* — together, indivisible as one ....

Black out.

FINIS

AT LOVECRAFT'S GRAVE

On the Fiftieth Anniversary of Lovecraft's Death—March 15, 1987

1
That does not sleep
which can eternal lie,
yet Howard, "Old Gent," "Ech-Pei-El,"
Lovecraft who signed himself
"Grandpa" and "Theobaldus"
to his fans and correspondents
most assuredly sleeps here.

We drift into the vale of earth,
the gentle falls and slopes
of Swan Point Cemetery,
gather to remember and praise him

as the Seekonk with its silted memories
ribbons at the edge of vision.
The sculpted monuments
  of angels and Psyches
repeat the largesse
  of immortal promises —
not so for his simple stone
placed forty years too late
to help his absent-minded shade
come home.
               Yews and cedars
bluff Ides of March
with bitter green, droop branches
like soiled wigs, while honest
bare branches of a spreading beech
retell the long years' chase of sun,
the repeated losses of winter.
Which is the emblem of Lovecraft's sleep?
His life lays stripped
  as that sorrowed beech
  where his initials are carved
  (real or spurious?)
his nightmares the evergreens,
  lingering through seasons,
  harboring nightwing
  as readily as lark.

2

We stand about, a handful
swelling to nearly a hundred,
trying to envision his folded hands,
his hand-me-down Victorian suit,
wonder how much of his habiliments
have fed the indiscriminate hunger
  of the conquering worm,

his eye sockets empty and dry
   gone beyond dreaming
though we close ours and see
the tower of ageless Kadath,
the shark-infested ruins of Ponape,
the imaginal Providence
where he walked arm-in-arm
with Poe and his eccentric Helen.

Our Lovecraft, lord
of the midnight shudder,
eaten from within
by the gnawing shoggoth of poverty,
the Azathoth of squamous cancer,
the loneliness of Nyarlathotep,
drugged by nurses into the sleep
where dreaded night gaunts fly
and bent flutes warble
a twisted melody–
and yet he faced it stoically
   like a proud Roman,
   an 18th century gentleman.
Death came with burning eye
   and found him not trembling,
never recanting his cosmic vision,
waving away the white-collared cleric
   with a wan smile.

3
Hundreds of miles we came today
to pause and pay homage,
readers and scholars who have leafed
his books, studied his papers,
debated his sources and meanings,
tread in his footsteps in Gotham

and Boston and Federal Hill,
stood with a thrill
   at his one-time door.

In sorry, mean-spirited Providence
no plaque or marker reminds us of him.
His grandfather's estate an apartment house,
his mother's house vanished,
his last abode uprooted and moved
like an aimless chessman on street map,
as though the upright town
   with its sky-piercing steeples,
   mind-numbing priests,
would like to erase him.

A baby in mother's arms
intrudes on our reminiscing,
breaks Carl Johnson's eulogy
with gurgles and cries of
"R'lyeh! Wah! R'lyeh!"
(shunned name of the city of doom
where multi-tentacled Cthulhu
dictates his madhouse symphonies!)

As someone reads a Lovecraft sonnet
   the sun blinks off
behind a humped shoulder
   of cloud,

and the air turns cold,
   unnaturally cold
in a spell of seconds.
Earth reels beneath our feet
into the chasm of sunless
   space.

4
Ah! this is the moon's business,
or the work of a moonless night.
Should we not speak of him
   beneath the glimmer of Hyades,
the velvet pall of the void,
the primal ether in which the cosmos
whirls like a raft into maelstrom,
the vast interior spaces
   of Time and the Angles
where the gods as he knew them
   drool and chant?

But they will not permit us
  to assemble by night.
They seal the gates
  against our ghoulish
  intrusions,
pretend that the coffined dead
  cannot be heard
to turn in their neglected
  crypts, deny
that lingering essences
  drawn from the memories
of the living can take
  an evanescent life —
pale shadows of shadows,
  reflected gleams
from the dusty pane
  of a mausoleum,
glints from polished granite
  or marble,
a sliver of sourceless light
in the eye of an owl
  or a raven;

pretend we are not
  untuned yet powerful
  receivers of thought,
  transformers of vision,

as if we did not know
how night
  vibrates with poetry,
  eidolons plucked
from the minds of the dead.

Reporters and camera crews
take us in warily,
eye us for vampire teeth,
   chainsaws, machetes,
   jewelry and witches' teats,
wonder what crimes we lust
   beneath disguises
to perpetrate
   upon their babies,
   their wives,
   their altars.

We smile,
   keeping our secret of secrets,
how we are the gentle ones,
how terror
is our tightrope over life,
how we alone
   can comprehend
the smile behind the skull.

5

Later a golden moon lifts up,
swollen with age and memories,
passing the veined tree skyline,
leaving its double in Seekonk,
disc face scanning the city —
the antfarm of students on Thayer,
the tumult of traffic on Main,
the aimless stroll of dreamers,
dim lamps of insomniacs,
the empty, quiet graveyard
winking like a fellow consiprator
at the prince of night.

Dimly on obelisk
a third moon rises.
The offered flowers
against the headstone
quiver and part.

A teenaged boy,
backpack heavy
with horror books,
leaps over the wall,
eludes the sleepy
  patrol car,
comes to the grave,
hands shaking
frightened,
exultant,
hitch-hiked all day

waiting,
mouthing the words
of Necronomicon,
for a sign
that does not come

the clear night,
the giant moon
throbbing
as he chants:

That is not dead
which can eternal lie,
And with strange eons
even Death may die.

LOW TIDE

"The tide was flowing out horribly—exposing parts of the riverbed never before exposed to human sight...something descended to earth in a cloud of smoke, striking the Providence shore near Red Bridge...The watchers on the banks screamed in horror—'It has come—It has come at last!' and fled away into the deserted streets."—H.P. Lovecraft, letter dated May 21, 1920

"brisk off-shore winds pushed a lower than normal 'moon tide' even lower on Narragansett Bay...miring dozens of pleasure boats in a sea of mud...There are mechanics who say that in the 20 years they've been working here, they've never seen anything like it."—Providence Journal, September 18, 1986

The azure sea, the silt brown Seekonk,
the placid ebbing of suntides,
the contrary pull of the moon,
all form a subtle balancing act —
until accumulated rhythms
resolve in one great tug
at the sleeve of the world.
The sea withdraws, the shape
of the earth convulsed by gravity

as if the sentient waters
grown weary of poison and oil slicks,
bereft of the colloquy of whales,
shrugged into space.

Would not the war-hemmed
Mediterranean be more serene
refreshing the cracked canals of Mars?
Would not the North Atlantic,
brimful of nuclear submarines,

prefer to slip off the earth-edge weightless,
an unmissed flotilla of icebergs
writing their names in the velvet sky
as comet messengers of Chaos?

69

The Narragansett waters drop
as the ocean makes its getaway,
rivers run dry
to fill the falling shoreline.

Drawn from their sleep by the burning moon,
the people, a motley of coats and robes
and slippers, a clot of bicycles and skates,
drift down to the riverbank
to see the helplessly stranded boats
dangle from their moorings,
level with their anchors,
topsy-turvy on a forest of pilings,
sails drooping and torn,
their rotors exposed like genitals,
their captains perplexed and swearing.

The riverbed undulates with dying fish,
the wriggling of eels in the hardening mud,
the half-seen slurry of amphibians.
Around the base of the iron-red bridge,
the barrows of humanity emerge:
a tangle of cars and mattress springs,
the skeletons of suppressed babies,
a statue of the Holy Infant of Prague,
a well-preserved gangster in a steel drum,
a thousand soda bottles & aluminum cans,
and, standing up like autumn trees–
or some hideous joke of the fishes–
the unfurled frames of lost umbrellas.

Someone says the water will return,
Low tide out, high tide in, insists
the river and the bay and the sea

will repave themselves with reflected sky.
Then why should a fireball plummet down
into the sodden riverbed? They watch,
hoarding their fears in the windless midnight,
as steam subsides over the mud-lined crater.

A madman, barefoot, bearded, rag-robed
avers that the Kraaken is rising
from the noisome mud on the bottom–
He snatches a fisherman's lantern
and runs across the Red Bridge screaming
"It has come! It has come at last!"

The people hear a distant murmur. A child
goes rigid with the spasm of seizure.
A woman faints, and no one leans
to pick her up. It is a blur
of stumbling and clawing: a boy
is struck down cold for his bicycle,
a deaf girl trampled near a street light.
Men break the door of the great-domed church,
determined to pray out the end of the world,
encircled by Host and holy books.

Of course, it is only the tide returning,
the meteor a slap from the brittle stars.
Homesick and dizzy from errant flight,
the prodigal sea comes home.
The boats resume their proper angles.
The bay fills in, the river rises.
The elders of Angell Street will say
None of this ever happened.

THE SWAN POINT GHOUL

Two months have passed
since I stood here,
in magic circle at the Old Gent's
grave, honoring Lovecraft.
The place I chose to stand on —
an older plot by a pine tree —
has dropped by a foot or more,
its earth a moil of root-turn,
brown against green
of surrounding sod.

Did the coffin collapse,
   or was it removed
      by something
      that tunnels
beneath the gravebeds? —
some necrophagic mole-man,
sharp claws on spatulate fingers,
red eyes sheathed in reptile layerings,
teeth jagged and piercing,
its sense of smell infallible,
burrowing from vault to tomb,
to late night lap of pond water,
to daylong sleep in a bat cave.

Even as we stood here,
      speaking our words of praise,
      reading our innocent poems,
did March earth muffle
      the splinter of casket
      the tear of cloth,
the insistent feeding
of the Swan Point ghoul?

HEARING THE WENDIGO

There is a place
    where the winds meet howling
cold nights in frozen forest
    snapping the tree trunks
    in haste for their reunion.
Gone is the summer they brooded in,
    gone their autumn awakening.
Now at last they slide off glaciers,
    sail the spreading ice floes,
    hitch a ride with winter.
Great bears retreat and slumber,
    owls flee
        and whippoorwills shudder.
Whole herds of caribou
    stampede on the tundra.
The Indian nods and averts his eyes.
Only brave Orion watches
    as icy vectors collide in air.
Trees break like tent poles,
    earth sunders to craters
    beneath the giant foot stamps.
Birds rise to whirlwind updraft
    and come down bones and feathers.

I have not seen the Wendigo —
    the wind's collective consciousness,
    id proud and hammer-fisted —
    to see is to be plucked
    into the very eye of madness.
Yet I have felt its upward urge
    like hands beneath my shoulders,
    lifting and beckoning.
It says, *You dream of flying?*
    Then fly with me!

I answer *No,*
not with your hungry eye above me,
not with those teeth like roaring chain saws,
not with those pile-driving footsteps —

I too avert my eyes
    against the thing that summons me.
Screaming, the airborne smiter
    rips off the tops of conifers,
crushes a row of power line towers,
peppers the hillside with saurian tracks,

then leaps straight up at the Dog Star

as though its anger could crack the cosmos
as though the skybowl were not infinite,
and wind alone could touch the stars
    and eat them.

MAKER OF MONSTERS, MAKER OF GODS

A birthday poem for Frank Belknap Long

How cold the sphere where all the gods are dead,
How grim the prospect when the end seems near!
How few deny the soul in age's bed,
Not brave enough to risk another year

Outside the soothing balm of Paradise.
Yet who, I ask, brings you this message bright —
God's hooded broker or a devil wise
In promise, slavering to steal the light

Of your assumèd immortality?
Beware these masked intruders, all of them!
God's hall and Satan's hot locality
Are only a sly imposter's stratagem.

O poet good and gray, have courage still.
It matters not that gods retire or sleep.
We are their makers, who fashion or kill
as suits us, the gods of the air or deep.

No matter that your hand some days is frail.
That hand has summoned monsters and entwined
The earth's sublimest beauties in a tale.
No matter that the falling years unwind

The scroll or turn the pages dry and sère.
Poe's Bells and Gotham's storied steeples seize
Your spirit, soaring from Providence to here—
To ancient barks adrift Aegean breeze—

To Mars — to plains where gods and heroes dwell—
To charnel pit where ghoul contends with rat —
To limelit stage where vampire victims swell
Their last aortal ebb into a bat-

Deep hunger's all-consuming rage of red —
To aliens serene at crystalline gates —
Robots implacable — and demons dead
Until some stumbling fool reanimates

Hibernal horror with a taste for blood!
What need of god's incense and litanies
When every twist of pen compels the mud
To yield up dark, bat-winged epiphanies?

Fear not. Walk on among them unafraid.
Soul-snatching monsters are as dead as stone.
Hell's a blank corridor, its lord a shade.
TERROR you did not fear to tread alone

Shall buoy you up, with WONDER at its side.
Lovecraft you called the kindest man you knew,
Refused a priest the day before he died,
Said he preferred a sky where Night Gaunts flew.

That is not dead which leaps to poet's eye,
Where neither friends, nor gods, nor monsters die!

November 8, 1989

THE TREE
AT LOVECRAFT'S GRAVE

This solemn spreading beech
was once a perfect hemisphere
of waxy red-green foliage.
Now it is crippled and sere,
scarred by the pruning
    of diseased limbs,
trunk bared, a twisted bole
in the form of a petrified heart.
Its gnarled roots rake earth
with a death-row desperation.
Within another hollowed bole,
    (eye-socket for a Cyclops)
malignant mushrooms proliferate,
caps and stalks angled sunward.

The schoolboy gashes
    where fans have carved initials
    (their own and HPL's)
widen and blacken,
the once-proud limbs
    tattooed with NECRONOMICON,

HOWARD P. LOVECRAFT '99,
even a whole sentence
about the primacy of fear,
runes ruinous to a living monument.

Still, the furry beech-nuts fall like hail
to the delight of squirrels.
Still, the hard brown kernels issue forth,
each a perfect blueprint
of a perfect tree —

or have the roots, tasting the calcium
of author's bones, the humus rot
of eye and brain and memory
mutated the germ and flower anew
so that these seeds transcend
to sentience?

Gather these nuts, then,
and harvest them.
First they must hibernate
for the beech remembers glaciers.

Then they will germinate,
pale tentacles in search
of anchorage,
until the red-green engine
of stalk and leaf
is ready to catapult
into the sun-chase.

Will these trees move
of their own accord?
Will their root-claws crave blood

and the iron-rich earth
   of a crumbling grave?
Will the branches sway
   on windless nights?
Will fox-fires and will o' wisps
      paint impossible colors
on bud-ends and blossoms?
Will beech nuts burst
      to pale blue eyes
insomniac astronomers
with perfect vision,
counting the Pleaides,
numbering the galaxies.

And will they speak
      the patient sonnets
of their greater lifespans,
the long-arced lines
      their waving branches beat?

And somewhere within them,
      does *he* smile there,
transmuted poet and dreamer

subsumed into the eons?

Are those *his* thoughts
that make them tremble
   at every sunset,
his elder gods they fear
might swallow the sun
as it tosses in darkness?

Is he lord of their nightmares,
giving them Dread,
the obverse of the coin of Joy,
Fear, the companion of Wonder?

I regard the ailing tree,
   the modest gravestone.
The tree will die. The rain
   will wipe the letters clean.
Only the whispered words,
   the lines the fingers trace
from one yellowed book
   to another
endure —
I hold the burst nuts in one hand,
   a book of Lovecraft's tales in the other.
I study the cloudless, blue, deceptive sky,
the lie that conceals an infinity
   of screaming stars —

Oh, these roots have read him,
   they have read him.

HERE AT THE POINT

Secret transcript of a meeting of The Security
Committee of Swan Point Cemetery

Here at the Point
we tolerate no nonsense.
Let the word go out
to the security guards:

photographing the monuments
is not permitted,
especially at Lovecraft's grave.

Families spend thousands
to put these obelisks and stones,
statues and mausoleums
onto our grounds

to be seen here.
Here! not in some smelly
newspaper!

If artists show up
with paints and easels,
they can depict the foliage,
but not the monuments,
not the monuments!

Use your judgment, men.
If one of those Art Club Ladies
sets up to paint, just shoo
her off politely.

But if it's a RISD kid —
one of those green-haired,

snot-nosed spray painters
from the Design School,
a little ride over
to the *trespasser's shed*
might be in order.

TV crews
are absolutely prohibited —
escort them right back
to the outer gates.

As always, no picnicking!
No food or drink
whatsoever — last month
we had a whole family
eating at a graveside
(damn Armenians!).
We stopped that in a hurry.

You can't let up,
not for a moment.
Watch for those kids,
keep an eye peeled
for lurkers, and *couples*.

Matthewson here keeps a graph
of how many conundrums
we find, and where —

conundrums, you know,
those little rubber things —
disgusting!

This is a place of repose.
Repose. Why don't they get it?

No eating, no drinking,
no urinating, no fornicating,
no congregating.

Those Lovecraft fans
are the worst. Reading their poetry,
mouthing what rituals
we can only imagine —
what the hell is *Cthulhu fhthagn*, anyway?

That Rutherford person
and those evil twins
dressed up as Lovecraft
or monks or ravens —
they have to be stopped!
Why doesn't someone stop them?

And look at their clothes,
a mockery of the good clergy
with all that black — one man
was carrying a skull! Boys with black
fingernails, Jesus! Some of the women
may not even be women.
Just imagine what they do afterward!

This Halloween, we'll stop them.
We know they're dying
to get in here at night.
Gamwell, here,
will man the portable generator.
The flood lights are set up.
The Lovecraft plot
will be as bright as day.

Just let them try to come here naked,
bringing some animal, no doubt,
to sacrifice. Not on my watch!

You, Roby, you'll get
the use of the night goggles.
Anything bigger than a badger
moves, and you'll see it.
Blair and Potter, third shift
for the two of you,
and no sleeping! I want
to see those headlights everywhere.

Next year I'll ask the trustees
to approve a guard tower
with moveable searchlights,
but I doubt they'll find the money.
What else can we do?
The ghouls are everywhere.
We just want peace and quiet.
This is a proper cemetery
and my motto has always been
As below, so above.

THE EYE, THE MIND,
THE TENTACLE

1

It always begins with an eye,
primordial   lidless
at the center of everything,
seeing all and nothing —

the skid of electrons
   from orbit to orbit,
the tug of gases
gathering into star clouds,
the whole span
of the burning spectrum
from the heart-thump pulse
   of its own being
to the X-ray symphonies
     of black hole sharks.

For time beyond time
only the eye saw,
aloof at the center
of crawling Chaos,
piping its flutes
in shrill and random harmonies —
sight without sense or reason:
Azathoth!

2

Or does it begin with consciousness?
The moment a silicon slurry
in a viscous pool of hydrofluoric
acid forms a crystalline mantle
and spins a cortex of electrons
that suddenly erupts:

I am

Or when some feeble carbon form
shambles out of the ambiote sea
and has an inkling
of its sliver of being
to roar its own defiant:

I am

Unlike the eye,
it is mortal —
its molecules prone
to ionize and slip away,
its outer shell hungry
to absorb and process matter
to keep its ego fires ablaze.

It wants to be alone
in the cosmos,
spanning time and worlds,
growing until it encompasses
all by digesting all —

it is blind, but it feeds
on the consciousness of others:
Nyarlathotep!

3

Or does it begin
with a tentacle?
A blind and nearly brainless
    worm
comes to be and crawls
toward the warmth,
its razor teeth ready.

Beneath the sea
the tentacle is king,
from the stinging lace of jellyfish
to the empire of *Architeuthis*,
the giant squid
who prowl through the inky depths
in untold numbers
larger each year
and more numerous.

The more tentacles, the more
potential power to wield and win
dominion over the others,

not a chaos of wriggling arms
but a gigapoidal symphony,
a fugue beyond fuguing,
an eros of almost infinite
    gradations.

It sleeps because it wants to.
Its patient mind is solving
a theorem
whose solution will undo galaxies
and meld all consciousness
into one self-centered being
with but one eye,
one mind,
all things obedient to itself:

dread narcissist *Cthulhu*
in ruined R'lyeh,
may you never awaken!

4
The Eye sees all but knows nothing.
The Mind sees nothing, but feeds
    on other minds.
The Tentacle imagines it sees,
    makes love to itself,
    smites matter
      with its multitude of limbs,
    and calls its hungry devastation
       genius.
This poem spoke itself
    from a dark and nameless place,
inviting unthinkable sorcery:
      to join in self the eye of Azathoth,
    the cosmic awareness
       of Nyarlathotep,
    the daring of Cthulhu.
Titans in Tartarus, in guarded sleep —
a place so deep
an anvil could fall nine days from Hell
to reach its beginning —
even they would not dare this thing.

Do not say it, do not think it,
do not make these gods
aware of you.

—April 3, 2004
For the 11*th* *H.P. Lovecraft Memorial Program,*
Swan Point Cemetery, Providence RI

MIDNIGHT ON BENEFIT STREET, 1935

Three hundred years ago it was a footpath
winding among family grave plots —
moved, all moved —
    at least the *stones* were moved —
to pave and straighten.
Now it is a strange amalgam
    of mansions and squalor,
every other streetlight shattered,
every other doorway an entrance
    into delirium and vice.

John Brown's mansion lords over the street,
aloof at the end of its ponderous lawn,
high fence upon a looming wall
so you are always beneath it,
going about your business unnoticed.

Ear pressed to those stones,
what might you hear
beneath the slurry of earthworms,
what muffled groans and chain-clanks?
Or maybe the slip-slide of silk
upon the polished floor, the fumbling
for a long-forgotten key
to the snug merchant cabinets and cubbyholes
stuffed with lost bags of silver coins?

In the stillness of museum night,
the mummy shifts in its linens,
dry lips stirring in natrous dust.

The stolen Buddha's hand creaks slightly
as it regards its empty palm
with a wooden eye turned suddenly
as bright as the orb of a tiger.

Fireplaces puff out the acrid smoke
of exterminated forests, ash falls
in minute flakes, snow's prelude.

The brooding Athenaeum
thrusts up its temple front,
a vault where books
    and the ideas within them,
slumber untouched for decades.
tended by
    frowning priestesses.

A hurried shadow passes
    the darkened Armory,
with its faint air of rust
    and dampened sulphur.
Long past the freighting time,
    the railway tunnel
    beneath the street echoes
    the shout of a drunkard,
    then silence — no,
    not silence —
    the chittering of rats,
thousands down there
in nightly migration
between two rivers.

Does he linger now
before that house
whose double cellar doors
fronting the sidewalk,
where phosphorescent fungi
alarmed his boyhood visits,
and feral scurryings
bred nightmares
of things that gnawed
behind the wallpaper?

He keeps the Capitol in sight,
and overhead, a crescent moon,
and there! a scintillant Venus,
forming a triad with Regulus,
up in the lair of the Lion,
this night of all nights of the year.

And there, the steeple
    on distant Federal Hill,
St. John's, the Starry Wisdom place.
If only the worshipers knew
what secrets slept above them!

He passes, too, the house in red,
the garden of roses where Poe
first saw the Helen of Helens,
the dark-paned parlor of wooing,
the door that finally
    barred and denied him.

He looks down to the ruined waterfront,
past the Episcopal churchyard
to the silted river, the rotting wharves,
the sullen, silent warehouses
that once burst with silks and tea.
In one of those dim taverns Poe
recited "The Raven" for a whiskey.

Somewhere down there
in a Chinese alley
lay the way to Eldorado
or the Valley of Dreams —
but no, these are modern times —
there is nothing down there
but a wallet-snatch beating
for a solitary poet.
Howard Phillips Lovecraft
turns back homeward.

ALSO FROM THE POET'S PRESS

POET BARBARA A. HOLLAND RETURNS TO PRINT WITH THE 30th ANNIVERSARY EDITION OF HER LANDMARK COLLECTION, *CRISES OF REJUVENATION*!! The complete poetic cycle, *Crises of Rejuvenation*, originally published in two volumes in 1973-75, is now expanded and annotated by Brett Rutherford. These strange and wonderful poems, most inspired by the paintings of Surrealist Rene Magritte, were a vital part of the 1970s poetry scene in Manhattan. They are reprinted here complete, with notes based on interviews with the poet.

JOEL ALLEGRETTI'S *FATHER SILICON*. One of the most startling books of poetry since Baudelaire. Joel Allegretti, author of *The Plague Psalms*, has been up to no good since his first book, and this new books goes darker and deeper still, delving into such delicate topics as The Juggernaut, Mother Julian of Norwich, Eurydice as Greta Garbo, Nico, spiders, the Gallows Tree, the horrors of 9/11, and "Billy the Whore: An Encomium in 9 Infections." This 72-page paperback book is now available from our online bookstore.

BRETT RUTHERFORD: *THE GODS AS THEY ARE, ON THEIR PLANETS*. This huge 208-page new collection of Brett Rutherford's poems can be ordered for $19.95 from our on-line bookstore. The Providence-based poet has included in this book all the poems he has written and revised since his last big collection, *Poems from Providence*. More than 150 poems, new and revised, cover the gamut from supernatural whimsies to love poems and political satire. Rutherford has been called "equal parts Poe, Shelley, Lovecraft and Bradbury" but he is also something unique, a true neo-Romantic. Sections of the book include 11 new autumn poems in the ongoing *Anniversarium* cycle; nine new graveyard poems, a clump poems inspired by the fall of the Berlin wall; major revisions and expansions of the poet's early Pennsylvania poems originally published in the 1973 collection *The Pumpkined Heart*; 17 urgent and odd love poems; and a half-dozen po-

ems based on myth and legend, including a new scene written to be inserted in Sophocles' *Oedipus Rex*. The book also includes 18 pages of notes about the poems.

WHIPPOORWILL ROAD: THE COMPLETE SUPERNATURAL POETRY. Expanded third edition. This extraordinary 272-page paperback contains all of Brett Rutherford's supernatural poems, including 72 pages of new poems since 1998. Praised by Robert Bloch and Ray Bradbury, these may be the best supernatural poems of the 20th century. Order the print edition from our on-line bookstore. This book includes the complete "Things Seen in Graveyards" cycle, along with major poems embracing familiar monsters: Dracula, mummies, werewolves, Gorgons, and a hilarious autobiography by Fritz, the hunchback assistant from *Frankenstein*. Ranging from hilarity to stark horror, the book also includes all the poet's work related to horror master H.P. Lovecraft. Notes about the poems round out this major collection.

ORDER ON-LINE FROM
www.poetspress.org